YA

DID ANYTHING GOOD COME OUT OF

THE CIVIL WAR?

PHILIP STEELE

ROSEN
PUBLISHING®

New York

Published in 2016 by The Rosen Publishing Group, Inc.
29 East 21st Street, New York, NY 10010

Copyright © 2016 Wayland/The Rosen Publishing Group, Inc

First Edition

Library of Congress Cataloging-in-Publication Data

Steele, Philip, 1948–
Did anything good come out of the Civil War?/Philip Steele.
pages cm.—(Innovation through adversity)
Includes bibliographical references and index.
ISBN 978-1-5081-7074-7 (library bound)
1. United States—History—Civil War, 1861–1865—Influence—Juvenile literature. 2. United States—History—Civil War, 1861-1865—Technology—Juvenile literature. I. Title.
E468.9.S8528 2015
973.7—dc23

2015024633

Manufactured in the United States of America

The publisher would like to thank the following for their kind permission to reproduce their photographs:

Key: (t) top; (c) center; (b) bottom; (l) left; (r) right

The following images are public domain: Front Cover c, bl, br. Back Cover tl cl bl. Endpapers. 4–5c, 6bl br, 7tl, 8tl b, 9tl, 10bl, 10–11c, 11tr, 12cl b, 13tl, 14bl, 14–15c, 15tr, 16br, 17tr br, 18tl cl, 19tl cr br, 20tl, 20–21 b, 21tl br, 22tl, 23c, 24–25b, 25tr br, 26, 27tr cl br, 28tl, 28–29b, 29cl cr, 30tr, 31tr b, 32tl bl, 32–33c, 33cr br, 34br, 34–35c, 35tl cr br, 36tl, 36–37br, 37tl br, 38–39c, 39tr br, 40tl tc tr bl br, 41tl br, 42tl bl, 43tl cl, 44tl cl bl, 45tl cl b, 47b.

All other images istock.com unless otherwise indicated.
13 br Robert Lawton.

Every attempt has been made to clear copyright. Should there be any inadvertent omission, please apply to the publisher for rectification.

METRIC CONVERSION CHARTS

1 inch = 2.54 centimeters	1 mile = 1.609 kilometers
1 foot = 30.48 centimeters	1 cup = 250 milliliters
1 yard = .914 meters	1 ounce = 28 grams
1 square foot = .093 square meters	1 fluid ounce = 30 milliliters
1 square mile = 2.59 square kilometers	1 teaspoon = 5 milliliters
1 ton = .907 metric tons	1 tablespoon = 15 milliliters
1 pound = 454 grams	355 degrees F = 180 degrees Celsius

CONTENTS

AT GETTYSBURG

The year was 1863, and General Robert E. Lee had just won a big victory at Chancellorsville, Virginia. He now wanted to press ahead into enemy territory, and so he ordered his troops, numbering more than 70,000 men, to march north into Pennsylvania.

GETTYSBURG, PA

The Battle of Gettysburg in Pennsylvania was the Confederates' last major offensive in the Union states.

A NATION DIVIDED

Lee's troops may have been invaders, but they were not part of some foreign force. Both sides were Americans and this was a civil war, fought between the northern states of the Union and the rebel states of the southern Confederacy. The war divided families and friends, North and South, black and white.

"THIS HAS BEEN THE HARDEST CAMPAIGN THE ARMY OF THE POTOMAC EVER HAD... IT IS BEYOND THE POWER OF ME TO DESCRIBE A BATTLE FIELD..."

Sgt Calvin Haynes of the 125th New York Infantry, Union forces, describes Gettysburg in a letter to his wife, July 19, 1863.

TIMELINE OF THE BATTLE, 1863

JUNE 28
Confederate forces hear that the Union army has marched into Pennsylvania.

JUNE 30
Union cavalry scouts spot Confederate troops near Gettysburg.

JULY 1
The two forces meet. The Confederates gain the upper hand.

JULY 2
The second day of battle sees some of the fiercest fighting of the war.

THE TURNING POINT

The Confederate advance was stopped at Gettysburg, 35 miles (55 km) southwest of Harrisburg, Pennsylvania. The fighting lasted from July 1–3. For two days the battle raged over once peaceful farmland. The Confederate forces came under continuous fire from a new repeating gun, the Spencer carbine. On the third day the Confederate general George Edward Pickett led a 15,000-strong charge against 10,000 Union troops on Cemetery Ridge. They broke through, but were forced to retreat under heavy fire. This Confederate defeat would be a turning point in the American Civil War.

Once the fighting was finished, the battlefield was littered with the bodies of dead Union soldiers.

CASUALTIES

Gettysburg was the deadliest conflict in the history of the United States. Union casualties numbered more than 23,000 out of nearly 94,000 troops. More than 3,100 were killed. Confederate casualties were much the same, but with over 4,700 losses.

JULY 3
The Union troops turn the tide and emerge victorious on the third day.

JULY 5
Troops begin to leave Gettysburg.

JULY 13
The last of Lee's troops cross over the Potomac River back into Virginia

NOVEMBER 19
Lincoln delivers the Gettysburg Address at the dedication of a military cemetery.

THE STATES AT WAR

The USA was not yet a century old, but it was on the verge of tearing itself apart. One reason was that the North and the South had very different societies, customs and political aims. They also had conflicting economic interests.

NORTH AND SOUTH

By the mid-19th century, the northern states, which had abolished slavery by 1804, were increasingly industrial. Migrants from Europe poured into the growing cities, seeking work in factories. Northerners saw their states as the powerhouse of a growing nation. They voted for trade tariffs to protect their industries from European competition. The southern states were rural lands with large tobacco or cotton plantations, which still used slave labor. Southerners relied on free trade with Europe, so they opposed tariffs. The USA had gained vast new territories and settlers were pushing westwards into these lands. As the territories became recognized as states, the southerners wanted them to permit slavery. But many northerners opposed this for both moral and economic reasons.

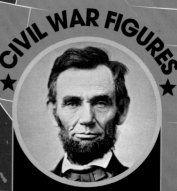

CIVIL WAR FIGURES

NAME: ABRAHAM LINCOLN

LIVED: 1809–1865

JOB: PRESIDENT OF THE USA

Having skilfully led the Union side in the Civil war, during which he issued the Emancipation Proclamation of 1863 that freed the country's slaves, Lincoln is one of the most celebrated US presidents. He was assassinated just as the war was coming to an end by the actor and Confederate supporter, John Wilkes Booth.

The cabinet of the Confederate States of America in 1861 with the president, Jefferson Davis, sitting in the front row, third from the right.

Slaves planting crops on a southern plantation during the Civil War.

SLAVERY AND ABOLITION

In 1857, the law courts ruled that the US Congress did not have federal powers to prohibit slavery in the new states. This ruling caused public anger and tension between the anti-slavery North and the pro-slavery South.

In November 1860, a new president, Abraham Lincoln, was elected. Lincoln was opposed to slavery. He was prepared for a gradual change of the system, but Southern states did not trust him and threatened to secede (withdraw from the Union). On February 8, 1861, seven states went ahead and proclaimed an independent nation, the Confederate States of America. Lincoln urged them to think again, but by April the two sides were at war.

The Warring States
Key to map:

The North: Population 22.3 million

 California (CA), Connecticut (CT), Illinois (IL), Indiana (IN), Iowa (IA), Kansas (KS), Maine (ME), Massachusetts (MA), Michigan (MI), Minnesota (MN), New Hampshire (NH), New Jersey (NJ), New York (NY), Ohio (OH), Oregon (OR), Pennsylvania (PA), Rhode Island (RI), Vermont (VT), Wisconsin (WI).

Slave-owning states of mixed loyalties that did not secede from the Union: Delaware (DE), Kentucky (KY), Maryland (MD), Missouri (MO).

The South: Population 9.1 million (including 3.5 million slaves)

 States that seceded before April 15, 1861: Alabama (AL), South Carolina (SC), Florida (FL), Georgia (GA), Louisiana (LA) Mississippi (MS), Texas (TX).

 States that seceded after April 15, 1861: Arkansas (AR), North Carolina (NC), Tennessee (TN), Virginia (VA).

"MY PARAMOUNT AIM IN THIS STRUGGLE IS TO SAVE THE UNION…"

US President Abraham Lincoln, *New York Times*, August 1862.

THE WAR BEGINS

Early on April 12, 1861, 5,500 Confederate rebels bombarded a Union garrison at Fort Sumter in the port of Charleston, South Carolina. The war had begun. President Lincoln called up 75,000 militia men and set up a naval blockade of the Southern coast.

CIVIL WAR FIGURES

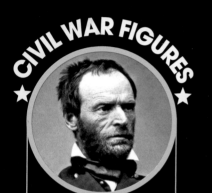

NAME: WILLIAM SHERMAN

LIVED: 1820–1891

JOB: UNION GENERAL

Second only to the commanding Union general, Ulysses S Grant, General Sherman was an accomplished and ruthless soldier. His 'March to the Sea' in late 1864, during which his troops laid waste to the state of Georgia, decisively swung the conflict in the Union's favor.

> "THE FIRING ON THAT FORT WILL INAUGURATE A CIVIL WAR GREATER THAN ANY THE WORLD HAS YET SEEN… YOU WILL LOSE US EVERY FRIEND AT THE NORTH. YOU WILL WANTONLY STRIKE A HORNET'S NEST WHICH EXTENDS FROM MOUNTAINS TO OCEAN."

Robert Toombs, Secretary of State for the Confederacy, writes to Confederate President Jefferson Davis, April 11, 1861.

1861

APRIL 12
Confederate forces attack Fort Sumter, South Carolina.

JULY 21
Battle of Bull Run, near Manassas, Virginia. Union forces retreat to Washington DC.

OCTOBER 21
Union troops are defeated at Ball's Bluff, Virginia, on the banks of the Potomac River.

Black soldiers from the 4th United States Colored Infantry who were assigned to guard Washington DC during the Civil War.

WHERE THE WAR WAS FOUGHT

The Civil War took place in two main areas known as theaters. The Western Theater ran from the Mississippi River to Georgia and the Carolinas, and included the heartlands of the Confederacy. The Union forces tried to win control of its rivers: the Mississippi, the Tennessee and the Cumberland. The Eastern Theater ranged over Virginia and West Virginia, Maryland and Pennsylvania. The Union capital at Washington DC and the Confederate capital at Richmond (from May 1861) were only 105 miles (170 km) apart.

CALLED TO FIGHT

The Union had much in its favor. It had twice as many soldiers as the Confederacy, as well as five times as many factories, most of the railways and greater access to weapons production. On the other hand, the South commanded great loyalty and had some first-rate military commanders. It hoped – in vain – to win support from the foreign countries with which it traded, such as Great Britain. Both sides ended up conscripting men into service, the South in 1862 and the North in 1863. The Union allowed people to pay money in place of military service, and this was seen to be unfair, causing riots in New York City. The Confederates used African American troops as slaves and servants, but not as soldiers. The North enlisted them from 1862, and in July 1863 the volunteers of the 54th Massachusetts Colored Infantry became the first of 179,000 African Americans to fight in combat.

President Lincoln (center) shown with Allan Pinkerton, the head of the US Intelligence Service (left) and Major General John A McClernand (right) in1862.

1862

JANUARY 19
The Union claims victory at Mill Springs, Kentucky.

APRIL 6–7
Union General Ulysses S. Grant secures victory at the Battle of Shiloh, Tennessee.

DECEMBER 13
Lee's forces defeat the Union at the Battle of Fredericksburg, Virginia.

THE TIDE TURNS

The war was fought on rivers and seas as well as in towns and the country. The Confederates' strength lay in their home territory. The Union troops suffered many early setbacks, only gaining the upper hand after the Battle of Gettysburg in July 1863. Even then, it still took them the best part of two more years to conquer the south.

"THE UTTER DESTRUCTION OF (GEORGIA'S) ROADS, HOUSES AND PEOPLE WILL CRIPPLE THEIR MILITARY RESOURCES. I CAN MAKE THIS MARCH, AND MAKE GEORGIA HOWL."

Union General William T Sherman, September 9, 1864.

THE POLITICS

The man chosen as Confederate President in 1861 was a soldier and pro-slavery politician called Jefferson Davis. He was not an inspiring leader and failed to keep a grip on the southern economy.

As Union President, Abraham Lincoln was tireless in his command of the troops, but politically cautious. At first, he did not make ending slavery his main aim, fearing that more states might join the rebels. However on

January 1, 1863, Lincoln's Emancipation Proclamation came into force, an order that the slaves in the rebel states should be regarded as free. This was now a war of liberation.

There were more than 28,000 casualties on both sides following the fierce Battle of the Wilderness from May 5–7, 1864.

1863

1864

JULY 1–3
The Battle of Gettysburg halts the Confederate advance.

JULY 4
Vicksburg, Mississippi, falls to the Union after a long siege.

MARCH 10
Start of the Union forces' Red River campaign to attack the deep South.

AUGUST 5
Confederate forces are defeated in the naval battle of Mobile Bay.

THE MARCH TO THE SEA

By late 1864 Union troops under General Sherman were marching through Georgia to the coast, destroying Confederate military bases, railways and factories as they went. The Confederacy was in deep trouble. In the winter of 1865, much of the South was starving and in ruins. Richmond fell to the Union on April 3.

Entrenched Union soldiers before the Battle of Chancellorsville, May 3, 1863.

CIVIL WAR FIGURES

NAME: JEFFERSON DAVIS

LIVED: 1822–1885

JOB: CONFEDERATE LEADER

As a former soldier and US Secretary for War – not to mention a plantation owner with 100 slaves – President Davis seemed the perfect candidate to lead the South to victory. But he was unable to overcome the richer, more populous and more industrialized North. He was captured and imprisoned after the South's defeat, but released two years later. He never held political office again.

1865

NOVEMBER 16
General Sherman's troops begin their March to the Sea through Georgia, creating havoc.

FEBRUARY 17
The Confederate stronghold of Columbia, South Carolina, is destroyed by fire.

APRIL 9
Confederate General Robert E Lee surrenders to Union Lt General Ulysses S Grant at Appomattox.

END AND AFTERMATH

On April 9, 1865, after heavy fighting at the Battle of Appomattox Courthouse, in Virginia, the Confederate General Robert E. Lee finally surrendered to Lt General Ulysses S Grant, the Union commander. The other Confederate troops surrendered in the months that followed. The day had come at last when, in the words of a popular song of 1863, 'Johnny comes marching home again'.

CIVIL WAR FIGURES

NAME: ULYSSES S GRANT

LIVED: 1822–1885

JOB: UNION GENERAL AND PRESIDENT OF THE USA

As the head of the army, Grant led the Union forces to victory in the Civil War. Elected president in 1868, he pushed forwards the Reconstruction reforms, seeing the first African Americans elected to political office. However the second half of his term was overshadowed by some very severe economic problems.

THE RECONSTRUCTION

The 13th Amendment to the US Constitution, abolishing slavery, was adopted in 1865. It was part of a wider program called Reconstruction designed to reunite the nation. But there were political clashes between those who wanted to protect the rights won by African Americans and those who wanted to return to the old way of life. The southerners resented the 'Yankees' (northerners) who came south to rebuild, accusing them of profiting from their misfortunes. Many in the North also opposed the Reconstruction program, and it was ended in 1877.

General Robert E. Lee (left) surrenders to General Grant (right) at Appomattox, 1865.

Lincoln's funeral procession on Pennsylvania Avenue, Washington DC.

AMERICAN CIVIL WAR

April 12, 1861 – May 9, 1865

Union forces
Strength: 2,100,000
Wounded: 282,000
Total dead: 365,000

Confederate forces
Strength: 1,064,000
Wounded: 137,000
Total dead: 260,000

Total losses in the Civil War about 625,000

COMPARISONS

US losses World War I (1914–1918) 116,516

US losses World War II (1939–1945) 405,399

US losses Vietnam War (1955–1975) 58,209

THE DEATH OF LINCOLN

Just five days after the surrender of Robert E Lee, Abraham Lincoln went to the theater in Washington DC to see a play called *Our American Cousin*. It was Good Friday, April 14, 1865. There, the president was shot by a well-known actor called John Wilkes Booth, one of a group of Confederate sympathizers who were plotting to kill the Union's leaders. Lincoln died the next day. Millions attended his funeral procession in Washington DC and lined the track as his coffin was taken by rail to Springfield, Illinois. Vice-President Andrew Johnson (1808–1875), became President in his place. He was succeeded by the former Civil War general, Ulysses S Grant, in 1869.

It seems strange to talk about 'good' things coming from a war that turned Americans against Americans and cost thousands of lives. But the American Civil War decided the future of the United States. The most important result of the Union's victory was the abolition of slavery. It also saw new 'fairer' rules of war introduced, provided a boost to women's rights and, like most wars, brought new medical and technological advances. However, the war's legacy was also lasting tension between the North and South, who would enjoy very different economic fortunes, deep-seated racial tensions, and disagreement about how a federal government should work. This book will examine the outcomes, both good and bad, expected and unexpected, of the Civil War.

★ HOW CAN ANYTHING GOOD COME OUT OF WAR? ★

13

WHOSE FREEDOM?

One of the early mottos of the United States was *E pluribus unum*, Latin words which mean. 'Out of the many, one'. Just what that meant in practice was an argument at the root of the Civil War. Was the USA a loose federation of states, each of which had an absolute right to decide their own policies? Or did the federal government in Washington DC have the right to overrule state laws?

THE BUILDING OF THE NATION

The victory of the Union confirmed that, although each state still had its own legislature, the ultimate power lay in Washington DC. There is little doubt that the Union's policies of unity, industrialization and economic growth helped the USA become, in the following century, the world's greatest political and economic power. Lincoln's ideal of 'government of the people, by the people, for the people' claimed the principles of democracy and freedom for the Union. But the Confederate General Robert E. Lee warned that if America became a vast, unified power in the world, it would no longer be true to its founding principles.

CIVIL WAR FIGURES

NAME: ROBERT E. LEE
LIVED: 1807–1870
JOB: CONFEDERATE GENERAL

The supreme commander of the Confederate army, Lee entered the war reluctantly. Having served in the US army, he wanted his country to remain intact. He won numerous battles for the South but was unable to overcome the North's advantages of manpower and industry. After the war he supported the Reconstruction.

"THE CONSOLIDATION OF THE STATES INTO ONE VAST REPUBLIC, SURE TO BE AGGRESSIVE ABROAD AND DESPOTIC AT HOME, WILL BE THE CERTAIN PRECURSOR OF RUIN WHICH HAS OVERWHELMED ALL THAT PRECEDED IT."

Robert E. Lee writes to the English historian Lord Acton, December 15, 1866.

BIG GOVERNMENT?

Lincoln hoped that the bitter divisions of the Civil War would soon heal, but questions about federal power still divide many Americans today. Most are strong supporters of federal government, as many were during the Civil War. However, others, not just in the South, share a distrust of Washington DC and the federal system, and this may also be a legacy of the Civil

Members of the Tea Party hold a rally in Washington DC.

War. Many conservative Republicans want to limit the part played by the federal state, reduce taxation and support the free market. Many libertarians believe that federal powers too often restrict the freedom of the individual. Members of the modern Tea Party movement are inspired by the Boston Tea Party, a protest against British rule in 1773, but perhaps they have more in common with the Confederate rebels of 1861.

Extreme hatred of federal government was the motive for the Oklahoma City bombing in 1995, which killed 168 people.

FLAGS AND SYMBOLS

The old 'battle flag' of the Confederacy is still flown in the USA, and also appears on car bumper stickers and T-shirts. It is often unclear whether people are flying it for reasons of history and heritage, as a symbol of rebellion, or to show their support for racism against African Americans. The flag still arouses powerful feelings today, both inspiring pride and causing offence.

AN END TO SLAVERY

Debates about the way a nation is organized are essential in any democracy. However, the arguments about the powers of federal government that sparked off the Civil War were closely linked to an even more important question, that of slavery.

CREATED EQUAL?

Slavery was the great flaw in the American political system. The US Declaration of Independence of 1776 had stated: 'We hold these truths to be self-evident, that all men are created equal.' Yet millions of African Americans were being deprived of their freedom and human rights and often suffering from cruel punishment.

Illustration showing escaped slaves being recaptured just before the Civil War (1853).

The three centuries of the slave trade between West Africa and the Americas were a horrific example of inhumanity. Shackled and packed into ships, millions of Africans died just crossing the Atlantic. The survivors were taken to North and South America and to the Caribbean islands. There they were separated from their families, auctioned, sold and branded like cattle.

Slavery was abolished in the British Empire in 1833, and since the early 1800s, the campaign for abolition in the USA had grown stronger. It was inevitable that slavery would become the great issue of the Civil War.

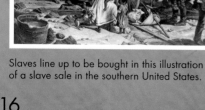

Slaves line up to be bought in this illustration of a slave sale in the southern United States.

CIVIL WAR FIGURES

NAME: HARRIET TUBMAN

LIVED: 1822–1913

JOB: UNION SPY

Born a southern Slave, Harriet escaped from her owners to the North in 1849. Afterwards, she returned several times to the South where she helped to free more than 70 of her family and friends. She acted as a spy for the Union in the Civil War and afterwards campaigned for the right for women to vote.

> **"I LOOKED AT MY HANDS, TO SEE IF I WAS THE SAME PERSON NOW THAT I WAS FREE. THERE WAS SUCH A GLORY OVER EVERYTHING; THE SUN CAME LIKE GOLD THROUGH THE TREES, AND OVER THE FIELDS, AND I FELT LIKE I WAS IN HEAVEN."**
>
> Harriet Tubman, escaped slave and abolitionist.

EQUAL RIGHTS

Some southerners opposed slavery. Some northerners supported it. Both of the main political parties were split on the issue. So the passing of the 13th Amendment to the US Constitution in the final years of the war was a great achievement. The abolition of slavery was undoubtedly the most important outcome of the war. The tragedy was that it was only achieved through such terrible bloodshed and destruction.

A 14th Amendment to the the Constitution was passed in 1868, also as part of the Reconstruction program. It was intended to give former slaves citizenship rights and equality before the law. The amendment faced great opposition, and not just in the South. A 15th Amendment, the last of the Reconstruction era, was passed in 1870. It declared that a federal or state government had to allow any citizen to vote, 'regardless of their race, color, or previous condition of servitude'.

These amendments were landmarks for the progress of human rights around the world. However, there was a problem. Many white Americans were determined that no former slaves should ever be treated as their equals.

The former slave and abolition campaigner Sojourner Truth, who recruited black troops for the Union side in the Civil War.

PROGRESS DENIED

The granting of civil rights to all African Americans was an important principle. However, these precious, hard-won amendments to the US Constitution were often ignored or evaded, as the former slave states set up one level of law for whites and another for blacks. Many of the whites who held power believed that African Americans were naturally inferior. The same racist attitudes were common at that time in Europe's overseas empires.

★ BLACK CODES

Laws known as 'Black Codes' began to be passed by state governments in 1865–1866. They made it possible for poor vagrants, many of them black, to be picked up and forced to work against their will. To prevent African Americans from voting, the lawmakers made up all sorts of restrictions. They brought in a poll tax, so that the public had to pay a tax in order to vote. How many ex-slaves could afford that? They said only people who could read and write could vote – even though most slaves had never received any form of education. African Americans were eventually allowed to vote in 1869.

★ SEGREGATION AND RACE HATRED

Southern laws brought in segregation, keeping the races apart in public spaces, schools and restaurants. These were known as 'Jim Crow' laws, after an African American stereotype mocked in minstrel shows. A US federal law of 1875, the Civil Rights Act, banned segregation, but it was overturned by the US Supreme Court in 1883. A secret racist organization, the Ku Klux Klan, was also founded in the South during the Reconstruction Years. Its members disguised themselves in robes and hoods (left), and terrorized African American families, burning down homes, murdering and lynching.

★ A BLACK PRESIDENT

In 2009, an African American, Barack Obama (left), was elected as US President. This revealed the huge political and social change that had swept across the United States since the 1960s. But today there are still concerns that too many young African Americans encounter social injustice. The burning issues of justice raised in the American Civil War are still relevant today.

★ THE DREAM OF FREEDOM

The National Association for the Advancement of Colored People (NAACP) was founded in 1909 to challenge the Black Codes in the law courts and to push for true equality.
It marked the start of a long campaign for African American civil rights. This came to a head in the 1950s and 60s when African Americans challenged segregation across the South. In 1963, a hundred years after the Civil War, a huge protest march on Washington DC, led by the non-violent campaigner Dr. Martin Luther King Jr., brought a call for change that the federal government could no longer ignore. A new Civil Rights Act was passed in 1964. More radical and sometimes violent protests continued into the 1970s.

"THE LAW ON THE SIDE OF FREEDOM IS OF GREAT ADVANTAGE ONLY WHEN THERE IS POWER TO MAKE THAT LAW RESPECTED."

Frederick Douglass, *Life and Times of Frederick Douglass* (1881)

Rosa Parks, whose refusal to give up her seat on a bus to a white passenger in 1955 made her a Civil Rights icon.

Dr. Martin Luther King Jr., one of the main leaders of the US Civil Rights movement.

★ NATIVE AMERICANS ★

What did the American Civil War mean for Native Americans? Nearly 29,000 of them fought in the war and it was a Seneca chief, General Ely S Parker (right), also known as Donehogawa, who drew up the surrender document that Lee signed at Appomattox. Most tribes supported the Union but some, such as the Creek and Choctaw, who were themselves slave-owners, sided with the Confederacy. Some of the Native Americans who fought in the war hoped to win a better deal from the government and perhaps a change of the policies that were forever driving them off their lands. As it happened, the Union government decided to speed up settlement of the Indian lands to the west after the conflict. Both Native Americans and African Americans suffered from discrimination and racism, but their legal status was different. The former were regarded as members of 'tribal nations' and were not granted US citizenship until 1924.

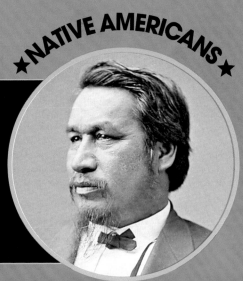

THE RULES OF WAR

The big political questions of the Civil War were about the nature of government, freedom, human rights and civil rights. These questions were not always resolved, and the war did not deliver justice for all. But other questions were also being asked. How should wars be carried out? What were the rules of fighting?

A portrait and dog tag (identity necklace) of the Union soldier, Alvin B Williams, who enlisted on August 11, 1862, aged 18, and was killed in battle on May 11, 1864.

THE LIEBER CODE

In 1863, President Lincoln issued 'Instructions for the Government of Armies of the United States in the Field'. This became known as the Lieber Code, because it was written by a German-American legal expert called Franz Lieber. Lieber had himself fought in Europe in his youth, and had sons fighting on both sides of the Civil War, so he was particularly concerned to see that the fighting was as 'fair' as possible.

"ART. 16. MILITARY NECESSITY DOES NOT ADMIT OF CRUELTY – THAT IS, THE INFLICTION OF SUFFERING FOR THE SAKE OF SUFFERING OR FOR REVENGE, NOR OF MAIMING OR WOUNDING EXCEPT IN FIGHT, NOR OF TORTURE TO EXTORT CONFESSIONS..."

From the Lieber Code, Section 1 Article 16 (1863).

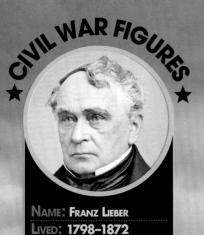

CIVIL WAR FIGURES

★ ★

NAME: FRANZ LIEBER
LIVED: 1798–1872
JOB: CODE CREATOR

Born in Berlin, Lieber fought in both the Napoleonic War in 1815 and the Greek War of Independence in 1821. In 1827, he moved to the USA, where he became a university professor and a legal scholar. Despite living in South Carolina, he supported the North in the Civil War, during which he wrote his influential legal code.

ETHICAL WARFARE

The Lieber Code ruled that poisons and torture were unacceptable in warfare, and laid out terms for the treatment of prisoners of war, spies and civilians. The Code was largely ignored by General Sherman on his 'March to the Sea', the campaign that took him across Georgia from Atlanta to the port of Savannah during the Civil War, but in later conflicts it was used as the basis for war crimes trials. Most importantly, it inspired international conferences and laws on warfare, such as the Hague Conventions of 1899 and 1907 and the Geneva Conventions of the 20th century.

General Sherman's troops (above) tear up the railroad during the March to the Sea to increase the suffering of the local people. They also chopped down telegraph poles and took crops and livestock (left) to make it harder for the Confederates to continue fighting the war.

A NEW AMERICA

The Civil War had been about economics as well as politics. After the war, the northern economy boomed but the South still suffered for many years to come. The economic program of Reconstruction failed.

The city of Charleston, South Carolina, lies in ruins after the war.

OUT OF THE RUINS...

The Civil War years had devastated the Confederate states. Their cities and factories lay in ruins, and railway tracks had been torn up. In a land where wealth was measured by the number of slaves employed on a plantation, abolition meant financial ruin for many.

Banks collapsed, and the war bonds that people had bought to support the Confederate government had lost their value. Cotton exports had declined as British India and Egypt moved into the market. For the rest of the century and into the next, the South lagged behind the rest of the United States. It still relied on farming, and attracted little money for industrial investment.

★ SHARE CROPPING ★

The booming North – a steelworks in Pittsburgh, Pennsylvania, in the late 19th century.

Many former slaves and even more poor whites, unable to own their own land, now lived by sharecropping. A landowner contracted them to farm a plot of land in return for a share of the profits. It was a risky way to make a living, and some said the grinding poverty was little better than slavery.

"THE SAID COOPER HUGHS FREEDMAN WITH HIS WIFE AND ONE OTHER WOMAN, AND THE SAID CHARLES ROBERTS WITH HIS WIFE HANNAH AND ONE BOY ARE TO WORK ON SAID FARM AND TO CULTIVATE FORTY ACRES IN CORN AND TWENTY ACRES IN COTTON"

From a Mississippi sharecropper's contract, 1867.

POOR SOUTH, RICH NORTH

Some industries did develop in the old Confederacy. Coal from Virginia, Kentucky and Tennessee supplied northern industries, and Birmingham, Alabama, founded in 1871, became a big industrial center. Former farm workers, including many African Americans, came to work in its iron and steel works. In the North, the economy grew quickly after the war and soon industrial cities sprawled across the land. The North was linked to the new farming areas of the Midwest and West and its factories processed food for the growing population. From 1865 onwards, livestock was brought by rail to the stockyards of Chicago, which became the meat-packing capital of the world. However, life for factory workers in the cities was often tough. In the 1870s, and again in the 1890s, there were economic crises that resulted in high unemployment.

23

PEOPLE ON THE MOVE

The 19th century was a time of great social change when people were on the move around the world and across North America. The American Civil War was at the center of many of these migrations.

IMMIGRATION

The number of Europeans settling in the United States had greatly increased in the years before the Civil War. In 1830, just 1.6 percent of the population was foreign born. By 1850, the figure was 9.7 percent. Many of the immigrants were fleeing poverty or hunger, such as the 781,000 Irish who left Ireland because of the terrible famine of 1845–1849. Other immigrants were escaping political or religious persecution, or simply seeking a new start. It was this wave of immigration that provided the workers for the North's Industrial Revolution, challenging the slave-based plantation economy of the South. Many of the newcomers fought for the Union in the Civil War.

After the Civil War there was a massive surge in migration from Europe, as a result of the industrial boom in the North. Millions of Italians, Germans, Scandinavians and Slavs poured across the Atlantic Ocean.

WESTWARD MIGRATION

In 1862, Abraham Lincoln signed the Homestead Act, which offered land grants to new settlers, including freed slaves, in the lands to the west where they set up small farms and made new lives for themselves. The offer was not open to people who had joined the Confederate army. As settlers and migrants travelled west, Lincoln's law helped to transform North America and create the modern USA.

Settlers crossed America in huge wagon trains, carrying everything they owned to start a new life in the west.

In 1866, during Reconstruction, a Southern Homestead Act was passed to allow freed slaves to move on to land that they could farm. However some of the land was of poor quality and the settlers risked racist attacks, leading to the law being repealed in 1877. Some African Americans moved to the South's new urban centers, while others headed northwards. In time, this became a massive population shift with 1.6 million African Africans moving to the North between 1910–1930.

★ EXPANDING NATION ★

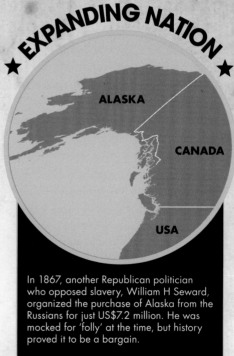

ALASKA

CANADA

USA

In 1867, another Republican politician who opposed slavery, William H Seward, organized the purchase of Alaska from the Russians for just US$7.2 million. He was mocked for 'folly' at the time, but history proved it to be a bargain.

> **"NOW IS A VERY FAVORABLE TIME TO COME TO AMERICA FOR ALL KINDS OF IMMIGRANTS SINCE THE ARMY HAS ABSORBED A CONSIDERABLE NUMBER OF THE COUNTRY'S WORK FORCE."**
>
> Norwegian ship's captain Knud Skjelsvig, writing home in 1862.

Italian immigrants fill the streets in New York City's 'Little Italy' district in around 1900.

The actual check used by the US to purchase Alaska from Russia.

WOMEN AND THE WAR

The anti-slavery movement and the Civil War both had a great impact on the role of women in American society. Middle class women were no longer stuck at home, but were out and about doing practical and useful work in the community.

Nurses and officers of the US Sanitary Commission in northern Virginia, where they tended to the wounded after the Battle of the Wilderness, May 1864.

NURSES

During the war, many women in both the North and the South volunteered as nurses. Some of them were inspired by the work of the English nursing pioneer Florence Nightingale in the Crimean War (1853–1856). A US Sanitary Commission was founded in 1861 and its Superintendent of Nursing, Dorothea Dix, convinced doctors of the need for women to carry out important work in hospitals. Women also raised funds, made uniforms, worked as cooks and laundry staff. African American women played an important part on the Union side.

> **"I COULD ONLY THANK GOD THAT I WAS FREE AND COULD GO FORWARD AND WORK, AND I WAS NOT OBLIGED TO STAY AT HOME AND WEEP."**
>
> Sarah Edmonds Seelye, who served with the 2nd Michigan Infantry as Franklin Flint Thompson.

> **"IN THE EARLY ANTI-SLAVERY CONVENTIONS, THE BROAD PRINCIPLES OF HUMAN RIGHTS WERE SO EXHAUSTIVELY DISCUSSED, JUSTICE, LIBERTY, AND EQUALITY, SO CLEARLY TAUGHT, THAT THE WOMEN WHO CROWDED TO LISTEN READILY LEARNED THE LESSON OF FREEDOM FOR THEMSELVES."**

From *History of Woman Suffrage* by Elizabeth Cady Stanton and others, New York, 1881.

FEMALE FIGHTERS

Neither side enlisted women as soldiers, but perhaps 400 to 750 women actually served in the Civil War disguised as men. After the war, the women who were homesteaders or living in remote territories had little choice but to lead a tough working life, and the same was true of women who were sharecropping in the South or sewing garments in sweatshops in the slums of New York City.

The women's rights movement in the United States was directly linked to the campaign against slavery, in which women played a leading part. A former slave named Sojourner Truth went on a speaking tour with the abolitionist George Thompson in 1851, and in the same year made a moving speech to the Ohio Women's Rights convention.

CIVIL WAR FIGURES

NAME: LOUISA MAY ALCOTT

LIVED: 1832–1888

JOB: AUTHOR AND CIVIL WAR NURSE

Author of the classic story *Little Women*, Alcott was the daughter of an activist on the Underground Railroad, a secret network dedicated to helping southern slaves escape to the North. A keen supporter of women's rights, she worked as nurse for the Union during the war. It was dangerous work. After six weeks, she caught typhoid and nearly died.

Frances Clalin disguised herself as a man (top image) called Jack Williams and fought in the Union army.

MEDICAL ADVANCES

Both sides in the American Civil War suffered terribly, but two-thirds of all casualties were from disease rather than bullets. At the time, people had a very limited understanding of infection. Medical advances are often made during wartime emergencies, and doctors can also sometimes learn useful lessons about public health. During the Civil War detailed medical records and reports were kept, and these helped doctors collect data for research.

★ BATTLEFIELD SURGERY

About 75 percent of surgical operations in the war involved the amputation of limbs to prevent the spread of gangrene. Neglect, long waiting times and crude surgery on the battlefield (left) were common. Army surgeons learned to act quickly and discovered just where to cut in relation to joints and the heart. The chances of survival improved greatly and became far higher than at civilian hospitals. Another improvement was in the stitching and sealing of chest wounds, a common cause of death in previous wars.

★ EMERGENCY SERVICES

American hospitals became much better organized as a result of the war. The delays in getting seriously wounded soldiers from the battlefield to hospital were dealt with by forming a horse-drawn ambulance service. This first served at the Battle of Antietam in 1862. In 1864, a US Ambulance Corps was created for the whole Union army.

In 1865, a civilian ambulance service was started at a hospital in Cincinnati, Ohio. In 1869, Edward Dalton, who had served as a Union surgeon, also set up a service in New York. The vehicles were fitted with medical kits and could be ready to leave within 30 seconds.

"OF ALL THE OFFICERS, THE SURGEON IS OFTEN THE ONE WHO REQUIRES MOST NERVE AND MOST COURAGE... UPON HIS COOLNESS AND JUDGMENT DEPEND THE LIVES OF A LARGE PROPORTION OF THE WOUNDED."

Harper's Weekly, July 12, 1862.

★ ANAESTHETICS

At the time, anaesthetics used to kill pain during operations included ether and chloroform. Chloroform was safer, as it did not catch fire – a possible risk in battlefield conditions. When the Union blockade stopped supplies of chloroform reaching the South, a Confederate surgeon called JJ Chisolm invented a small inhaler that used less chloroform more effectively. After the war, this type of inhaler was widely used for many years.

★ PLASTIC SURGERY

Plastic surgery to repair the damage of battle was pioneered during the Civil War by a skilled New York surgeon called Gurdon Buck (left). Buck was the first doctor to use photography in his clinical records.

Troops carry wounded Civil War soldiers on stretchers to a horse-drawn ambulance.

★ MALARIA ★

Both armies fighting in the warm and swampy South were plagued by tropical fevers, especially malaria. Doctors did not yet know that it was mosquitoes which spread the disease, but they did know that a useful medicine for treating it was quinine, made from the bark of the Cinchona tree. This was produced industrially for the Union forces, but supplies to the Confederates were halted by the blockade. They carried out scientific research into other plants that might be as effective, but had no success.

29

NEW TECHNOLOGIES

The Civil War was the first industrial war, making full use of trains and railways, factories and mass production. It saw great technical advances in weapons manufacture, which was the reason why so many soldiers were killed or wounded. The technology was remarkable, but no one could say that these methods of destroying human life were of great benefit to mankind.

FATAL FIREARMS

In the early days of the war, most troops used smooth-bore muskets. These could only load one bullet at a time and had a range of only about 750 ft (230 m). From 1861, many Union troops were equipped instead with the Springfield rifle, which could be accurate at a range of about 900 ft (270 m). The spiral grooves of the 'rifled' barrel span the bullet round, making it fast and accurate. It caused terrible wounds. More than a million Springfields were manufactured during the war. From 1863, repeating rifles were also introduced by the Union. These could fire several bullets before reloading was needed. The Spencer carbine could fire seven shots in 30 seconds.

The use of rifles at the Battle of Chickamauga in 1863 helped cause more than 34,000 casualties on both sides (the second highest total of the war) at this Confederate victory.

A Gattling gun, one of the deadly new weapons of the conflict.

RAPID FIRE

The Gatling field gun, an American invention of 1862, was used by Union troops in battle from 1864–1865. It was also fitted to boats. The Gatling was a forerunner of the modern machine gun. It had several barrels, which were rotated by using a hand crank. Cartridges were fed into the gun by gravity, allowing it to fire 200 rounds a minute.

"IT OCCURRED TO ME THAT IF I COULD INVENT A MACHINE A GUN – WHICH COULD BY ITS RAPIDITY OF FIRE, ENABLE ONE MAN TO DO AS MUCH BATTLE DUTY AS A HUNDRED, THAT IT WOULD, TO A LARGE EXTENT SUPERSEDE THE NECESSITY OF LARGE ARMIES, AND CONSEQUENTLY, EXPOSURE TO BATTLE AND DISEASE (WOULD) BE GREATLY DIMINISHED."

Wishful thinking from Richard Jordan Gatling (1818–1903), inventor of the Gatling gun.

WAR IN THE TRENCHES

New weapons changed the way battles were fought. The Civil War saw the start of trench warfare, in which troops dug into the ground to protect themselves. Trench warfare reappeared in World War I (1914–1918), with such a waste of young lives that it became a lasting symbol of the horrors of war. Another horrific development during the Civil War was the use of buried land mines that exploded when anyone stepped on them. These were designed by a Confederate Brigadier General named Gabriel J Rains.

Trenches at Fort Sedgewick where the Confederates dug in against the Union's superior firepower at the Petersburg campaign.

Union troops use a giant mortar known as 'The Dictator' at the Siege of Petersburg in 1864.

SEA TO AIR

The fighting in the Civil War didn't just take place on the battlefields. War was also waged at sea and, to a lesser extent, in the skies. As with weapons technology, these areas saw numerous innovations and improvements during the conflict as both sides sought the edge that would bring ultimate victory.

★ THE IRONCLAD REVOLUTION

Some of the ships in this war were not traditional wooden sailing vessels, but heavily armed steamships protected by armor. They were called ironclads. Some were riverboats, others built for the ocean. The first ironclad had been launched in France in 1859, but this new type of ship first saw military action in the US, in 1861. It was soon clear that ironclads were very effective against both other ships and coastal forts. They were packed with all sorts of new inventions. Ironclads evolved into the battleships of the 20th century.

The heavily armored gun turret of the USS *Monitor*.

★ SUBMARINE ATTACK ★

Both Union and Confederate navies were secretly working on designs for submarines. These were tested as early as 1861. The first ever successful submarine attack was made by the CSS *Hunley* in February 1864. This narrow tube of iron carried a crew of eight, who managed to ram a torpedo into the side of the USS *Housatonic*, a ship blockading the port of Charleston. The explosion caused the Union ship to sink in just five minutes – but the *Hunley* itself was destroyed in the attack. Submarines would play a very important military role in World Wars I and II, but they would also help future generations to explore the ocean floor and carry out valuable scientific research.

"THE AERONAUTIC TRAIN, CONSISTING OF FOUR ARMY WAGONS AND TWO GAS GENERATORS... ARRIVED A LITTLE AFTER NOON AND WERE PUT IN POSITION FOR INFLATING THE BALLOON. OUR OPERATIONS WERE IMPEDED FOR AN HOUR OR MORE BY OUR POSITION BEING SHELLED BY THE ENEMY, BUT NOTWITHSTANDING THIS THE BALLOON WAS READY AT 5.30 O'CLOCK... AT 3 O'CLOCK THE NEXT MORNING I ASCENDED AND REMAINED UP UNTIL AFTER DAYLIGHT, OBSERVING THE CAMP-FIRES AND NOTING THE MOVEMENTS OF THE ENEMY."

Official report from Thaddeus Lowe, head of the Union Army Balloon Corps, Yorktown, April 6, 1862.

★ THE WAR IN THE AIR

The Union forces pioneered the use of aerial reconnaissance in warfare. They did not yet have airplanes, but they did have hydrogen-filled balloons (right). These could move freely or be tethered to the ground by ropes. Balloonists could spy on enemy positions or direct troops in battle. It was already possible to telegraph information from the balloon back to land or sea. Balloons would play a useful role in future warfare and in scientific research, even after the invention of powered flight.

The first battle between armored warships took place on March 9, 1862 and involved the Confederate CSS *Virginia* (left) and the Union USS *Monitor* (right).

★ MINES AND TORPEDOES

Naval mines were used by both sides to blow up enemy ships on rivers and at sea (right). In those days, mines and underwater missiles were all called torpedoes. The Confederacy set up a special Torpedo Corps in Richmond, Virginia, aiming to attack the Union blockade. The Singer was the most common type of mine, made from iron, packed with gunpowder and moored in the water. It was designed to explode on contact. In all, 27 Union ships were mined during the war.

IDEAS AND INNOVATIONS

Wars are times of rapid change and urgent measures, and often bring about new and cheaper ways of producing goods, new inventions, processes or spin-offs, as well as huge improvements in transport and communication.

> ## "MAY GOD CONTINUE THE UNITY OF OUR COUNTRY AS THIS RAILROAD UNITES THE TWO GREAT OCEANS OF THE WORLD."
>
> Words engraved on the Golden Spike, which linked the final two segments of the Transcontinental Railroad, Promontary Summit, Utah, May 10, 1869.

A Union military locomotive in January 1865.

★ THE RAILROAD

The first steam locomotives were developed in Britain, but from the 1830s the United States began laying down railroads on a major scale. The Civil War was the first conflict in which railways played a big part. Trains were used to transport troops, supplies, fuel and food. Railways were often the targets of military action. They were important to both sides, but the industrialized North had more factories and workshops, and more miles of rail.

In 1862, as part of the Union's policy of pushing westwards, Lincoln went ahead with a plan to link the east and west of the country by rail, a move that had previously been blocked by Southern politicians. By 1869, a Transcontinental Railroad crossed the nation, a great feat of engineering. Railways changed America, encouraging settlement and economic development.

The ceremony for driving the 'Golden Spike' marking the completion of the Transcontinental Railroad on May 10, 1869.

★ STANDARD SIZES

The manufacture of uniforms for the Union soldiers during the Civil War increased the mass production and sale of ready-made clothing for men, in standard sizes.

A Union soldier in standard-issue uniform.

★ CANNED FOOD

Production of canned food increased by six times during the American Civil War, starting a major new industry. The sharp tin opener used by the troops was probably as dangerous as some of their weapons!

★ GREENBACKS

As for paying for all these goods, the Union government, short of cash, began printing paper money that was not backed up by a promise of repayment in metal coin. The first of these new dollar bills were called 'greenbacks', because one side was printed in green ink.

★ THE TELEGRAPH

In the 1840s and 50s, telegraph networks, which used electric signals to communicate messages in Morse Code, began spreading across the nation, linking businesses and communities. A US Military Telegraph Corps was set up in 1861 to make sure the war effort made the most of this new form of communication. It trained 1,200 new operators. Rigging up and operating telegraph lines under battle conditions was dangerous and difficult work, but it meant that President Lincoln could keep in direct contact with his officers. There was a special telegraph room in the Department of War, next to the White House.

Union soldiers reeling out wire prior to setting up an army telegraph in 1863.

35

MEDIA AND THE ARTS

The Civil War made the public hungry for news, and it was in these years that a revolution in journalism took place. It was made possible by two new inventions: the steam powered rotary press and the electric telegraph.

An enormous steam-powered rotary press turning out newspapers in 1864.

Photography brought home the human side of conflict. The faces stare back at us across the years.

THE LATEST NEWS

Invented in 1843, the steam-powered rotary press made it possible to print off millions of copies of a page in just one day. Newspaper printing increased by over four times in the years up to the war.

A second invention, the electric telegraph, was not just useful for the military, but also for reporters based with the armies. They could tell the public the very latest news as it happened. Some readers complained that articles written in the heat of battle were often garbled or misleading, and dashed off without proper reflection. Even so, up-to-date news reports sold newspapers.

The bulky camera and darkroom wagons of the Civil War photographer Sam A Cooley.

IMAGES OF WAR

The new gritty realism made it harder to take a romantic view of the slaughter. So too did the new art of photography. War artists recorded battlefield scenes quite realistically, but photographs told a deeper truth, and still move us today. We can see Lincoln or Lee as they really were, as well as troops, prisoners and dead bodies lying on the battlefield. Bulky camera and processing equipment had to be taken to the battlefields in horse-drawn wagons, but that did not put off the pioneering photographers and their assistants. The American Civil War was the first war to be widely photographed in this way.

"WE ARE LIVING HISTORY IN THESE EXCITING TIMES, AND THE HISTORIANS ARE THE NEWSPAPER WRITERS, REPORTERS AND CORRESPONDENTS."

Philadelphia Daily Evening Bulletin, 1861.

★ TELLING IT LIKE IT IS? ★

From the start of the war, there were worries about censorship. Would instant reporting by telegraph result in military secrets being given away? Would realistic photos, such as this one of battlefield dead, lose public support for the war? Voluntary guidelines were given to the press in 1861, but censorship was soon made much stricter. Generals were annoyed by inaccurate reporting, while censorship by the military often angered the press. The war saw the start of modern journalism.

MUSIC AND MARCHES

Listening to music is a good way of travelling back in time. By hearing the old tunes of the North and the South you can experience directly the atmosphere and the culture of the Civil War years. It is also fascinating for us today to track the many styles and moods of America's globally popular music back to that period.

The drum corps of the 30th Pennsylvania infantry division during the Civil War.

MUSIC ON THE BATTLEFIELD

Brass bands and drummers marched with the armies into battle, and buglers sounded signals. Many soldiers brought their own instruments to play in camp, including harmonicas, banjos or fiddles. The two sides would sometimes change the words of the enemy's songs, or compete with singing from the opposing lines. Some sentimental tunes, such as 'Home! Sweet Home!', were standards, loved by both sides.

A military bugle of the type used to sound signals and march soldiers into battle during the Civil War.

COMFORT FOR THE TROOPS

The invention of sound recording came in the years after the war, so music and singing were still performed live, whether in homes, churches, concert halls or army camps. The music helped to comfort both the troops in the field and those who waited for them back home. It might help the troops when marching into battle, or provide a patriotic anthem at a public ceremony.

★ FUSIONS ★

The Civil War and the migrations of the following years brought together all sorts of musical traditions – from Irish and Scottish dances to Spanish rhythms and Cajun songs with French words. The African American jazz and blues sounds of the South were taken to the northern cities during the later migrations, and in their turn would inspire rock 'n' roll in the 1950s. Black music would help to build bridges between the peoples of the USA where the politicians had so often failed.

'GLORY, GLORY, HALLELUJAH!'

The 1859 song 'Dixie' was an unofficial Confederate anthem, even though it was written in the North and was popular with Abraham Lincoln. It used mock African American accents and was sung at minstrel shows. 'Dixie' was a nickname for the South. 'The Battle Hymn of the Republic' (1861) was a stirring patriotic hymn, which took its tune from a Union marching song known as John Brown's Body. John Brown was a famous white abolitionist who had been hanged in 1859 for trying to start an armed slave uprising. A century later, songwriters were still composing songs about the war, such as Robbie Robertson's 'The Night They Drove Old Dixie Down', recorded by The Band in 1969 and by Joan Baez in 1971.

'John Brown's Body' was known simply as the 'John Brown Song!' when the words were first printed on this 1861 song sheet.

READING MATTERS

Frederick Douglass

Mark Twain

Walt Whitman

The abolition movement in the years before the war was encouraged by many books written by slaves who had escaped from the South. One of the best known was the *Narrative of the Life of Frederick Douglass* (1845). Douglass (1818–1895) was a great public speaker and campaigner. Books written after the war helped the nation to come to terms with what had happened.

CIVIL WAR FIGURES

In 1852, a white teacher born in Connecticut, Harriet Beecher Stowe, published a novel called *Uncle Tom's Cabin*, which told the story of a slave family. It was sentimental and full of African American stereotypes, such as Uncle Tom himself. But it sold 300,000 copies in the USA and a million in Britain, and perhaps did more than any other book to help abolition and the cause of the Union.

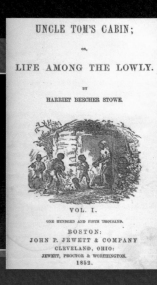

UNCLE TOM'S CABIN;

OR,

LIFE AMONG THE LOWLY.

BY

HARRIET BEECHER STOWE.

VOL. I.

ONE HUNDRED AND FIFTH THOUSAND.

BOSTON:
JOHN P. JEWETT & COMPANY
CLEVELAND, OHIO:
JEWETT, PROCTOR & WORTHINGTON.
1852.

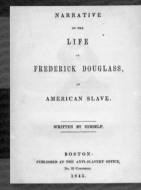

Title page of the *Narrative of the Life of Frederick Douglass.*

WRITERS AND THE WAR

The Civil War affected many of the greatest American writers and poets of the 19th century, such as Ralph Waldo Emerson, Emily Dickinson and Nathaniel Hawthorne. Mark Twain (1835–1910), a riverboat pilot on the Mississippi River when the war broke out, briefly served with a Confederate militia before deserting. The great poet and essay writer Walt Whitman (1819–1892) wrote a patriotic poem called 'Beat! Beat! Drums!' at the start of the war. When he went to look for his wounded brother, he was horrified by the bloodshed. He later wrote about the experience and for a time volunteered as a nurse. As the war went on, many writers became worried about the harsh realities of modern battle.

THE STORY GOES ON

After 1865, many soldiers and politicians wrote memoirs of the war, which were very widely read. Some of the best stories about the war were written many years later. In 1890, a former Union soldier called Ambrose Bierce wrote a brilliant short story called *An Occurrence at Owl Creek Bridge*, about a Confederate sympathizer from Alabama who is hanged during the Civil War. It was made into a film in 1962.

In 1895, the author Stephen Crane (1871–1900) published a realistic novel about the Civil War called *The Red Badge of Courage*, which looks at what we mean by heroism, fear and cowardice. It was filmed in 1951.

A slightly less realistic 1936 Civil War novel by Margaret Mitchell called *Gone with the Wind* sold 30 million copies worldwide. This was a romantic tale set in the plantations of Georgia and it told the story of a spoiled young woman called Scarlett O'Hara. The 1939 film was one of the most successful films in the history of US cinema.

> **"SO IT CAME TO PASS THAT AS HE TRUDGED FROM THE PLACE OF BLOOD AND WRATH HIS SOUL CHANGED."**
>
> Stephen Crane, *The Red Badge of Courage*, 1895.

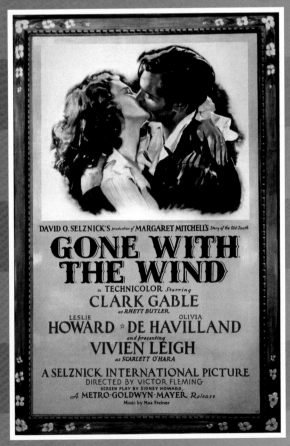

A poster for the 1939 film version of *Gone With the Wind*, starring Clark Gable and Vivien Leigh.

SO DID ANYTHING GOOD COME OUT OF THE CIVIL WAR?

THE BIG QUESTIONS

Around 625,000 people died in the Civil War, making it by far the deadliest conflict in US history. It achieved one unqualified good: the abolition of slavery. But that didn't end the problems for the reunited States. Many whites continued to resist equality for black people, and segregation continued in the South until the mid-20th century. The years after the war also saw increased westward expansion of the population – and increased conflict with Native Americans – as well as severe economic problems.

★ STILL NOT EQUAL

Although slavery was abolished and laws were passed allowing black people to vote and hold public office, race relations continued to be deeply problematic in the United States long after the Civil War. In much of the South, discrimination had become entrenched. Segregation laws were passed that forced black people to use different – and usually inferior – schools, restaurants and other public facilities from white people. Many laws were not overturned until Civil Rights leaders such as Dr. Martin Luther King Jr. (left) demanded change in the 1960s.

★ THE GETTYSBURG ADDRESS ★

Candles light up the graves of the fallen at the military cemetery in Gettysburg, Pennsylvania.

On November 19, 1863, President Lincoln delivered one of the most famous speeches in US history to mark the dedication of a cemetery to the Battle of Gettysburg fought earlier that year. In the speech, which was just a few minutes long, Lincoln (left, with his generals) called on the Union to continue the struggle to honor the men who had given their lives in battle.

★ BIG ECONOMY, BIG GOVERNMENT

The reunion of the states signalled the start of the USA's rise to become the world's greatest political and economic power. The North in particular experienced a major industrial boom after the war. The previously rural South also underwent some industrialization, but on a much smaller scale. Its economy would lag behind the North for decades to come. Many in the South were also distrustful of the big centralized government that emerged after the War. They felt that it had become too controlling and too willing to override the rights of individual states, something many had feared before the conflict. Campaigns against 'Big Government' still take place today.

★ EXPANDING THE NATION

Immigration to the United States exploded in the decades after the Civil War. Millions of people, particularly from Europe, took advantage of the USA's relaxed immigration laws and the advent of transatlantic steamship travel to start new lives for themselves. The population of the country's eastern cities swelled enormously. To counter this, legislation was passed encouraging people to settle in the new lands in the west. But this brought them into conflict with the Native Americans living there (left), who were often forced from their lands and onto reservations.

"WE HERE HIGHLY RESOLVE THAT THESE DEAD SHALL NOT HAVE DIED IN VAIN – THAT THIS NATION, UNDER GOD, SHALL HAVE A NEW BIRTH OF FREEDOM – AND THAT GOVERNMENT OF THE PEOPLE, BY THE PEOPLE, FOR THE PEOPLE, SHALL NOT PERISH FROM THE EARTH."

Abraham Lincoln's speech at Gettysburg, November 19, 1863.

POSITIVE EFFECTS OF THE CIVIL WAR

The story of the Civil War continues to fascinate, and influence, people into the 21st century. It had a profound effect on the subsequent development of both the USA and the rest of the world. Its main positive effect was, of course, the ending of slavery in the US. But the conflict brought about other beneficial changes, including medical and technological advances and new rules for warfare.

★ NEW AMENDMENTS

The passing of the 13th Amendment in 1865 may have ended slavery, but it was just the first step in trying to achieve racial equality in the USA – a process that is still underway today. Two further amendments, the 14th in 1868 and the 15th in 1870, were required to give former slaves US citizenship and the right to vote. The Civil Rights movement of the 1950s and 60s (left), led by Dr. Martin Luther King Jr., showed that racial discrimination remained entrenched in parts of the US long after the war was over.

★ NEW RULES OF WARFARE

Slavery wasn't the only major issue regarding the treatment of human beings to arise in the war. In 1863, the increasingly brutal nature of the campaign led President Lincoln to instruct a legal expert called Franz Lieber to draw up a new set of rules for the humane conduct of war. This Lieber Code laid out terms for the fair treatment of prisoners of war (left) and spies, and banned torture. It formed the basis for many later laws on warfare, such as the Geneva Convention.

★ WOMEN'S RIGHTS

The women's rights movement was given a great spur by the war. The fact that they contributed so much during the conflict, working as nurses and raising funds, but had so few rights, angered many women. The notions of human rights and equality raised by the war inspired many women to campaign for their own rights (left), particularly the right to vote. By the end of the century, some states had granted women the vote, which would be extended to the entire country after World War I.

★ MEDICAL ADVANCES

As with all conflicts where there is a sudden upsurge in injuries, the US Civil War saw several important medical advances. A new, more efficient inhaler for administering chloroform (a painkiller) was invented and improvements were made to several surgical procedures, including amputations and the stitching of wounds. But perhaps the most influential development was the creation of a horse-drawn ambulance service (left) for the Union army. Civilian ambulance services were introduced soon after the war.

★ TECHNOLOGICAL ADVANCES

The technological advances made during the war obviously included several new weapons, including rifles, icon-clad warships and the Gatling gun, the forerunner of the machine gun. But there were also more peaceful developments in the fields of transport (particularly railways, balloons [left] and submarines), photography (it was one of the first major conflicts to be photographed) and communications (including improvements to both the telegraph and newspaper printing).

In 1963, civil rights leader Dr. Martin Luther King Jr. led a march in Washington DC, to demand equal rights for black people.

"I HAVE A DREAM THAT ONE DAY THIS NATION WILL RISE UP AND LIVE OUT THE TRUE MEANING OF ITS CREED: 'WE HOLD THESE TRUTHS TO BE SELF-EVIDENT, THAT ALL MEN ARE CREATED EQUAL.' "

Dr. Martin Luther King Jr.'s speech at the Lincoln Memorial in Washington DC, August 28, 1963.

GLOSSARY

abolition
Putting an end to something, such as slavery.

amputate
To cut off a limb as a surgical procedure.

anaesthetics
Drugs used to reduce feeling or consciousness during surgery.

cabinet
The committee of ministers at the head of a government.

carbine
A short-barrelled rifle or musket.

casualty
Someone who has been killed or wounded in a battle.

civil rights
The rights of citizens to enjoy equality before the law.

civil war
A war fought between factions or regions within the same country.

conscription
Calling up civilians to fight in the armed services.

constitution
The body of laws that define how a nation is governed.

democracy
Rule by the people or by their freely elected representatives.

emancipation
Setting free.

federal
Representing the United States as a whole rather than individual states.

free trade
Trade that is free from duties and government controls.

gangrene
The dying off of living tissue through lack of blood supply.

inaugurate
To introduce or set up, or to formalize a new US presidency.

ironclad
An armor-plated warship.

legislature
A body which passes laws, such as an assembly, congress, or parliament.

libertarian
Emphasizing the freedom of the individual against the state.

migrant
Someone who moves from one place to another.

mine
A bomb, buried in soil or submerged in water, which explodes on contact.

Morse code
A system of signalling using dots, dashes and spaces.

mortar
A cannon with a short barrel which fires shells at a high angle.

paramount
Most important.

plantation
A large farm or estate growing a particular crop, such as cotton or tobacco.

racism
The belief that human beings can be divided into races, some of which are superior to others.

reconnaissance
Gaining information about the position of enemy troops.

segregation
A policy of keeping people of different races apart in public places.

slave labor
A workforce which is deprived of liberty and forced to labor for no reward,

telegraph
A system of electrical communication using a wire to send signals.

theater of war
The area in which fighting takes place.

trade tariffs Customs or duties imposed on imports or exports.

trench warfare
Using ditches dug in the soil as shelter from enemy fire and as a firing position.

war bonds
Debt issued by governments in order to raise money for military action.

FOR MORE INFORMATION

★ BOOKS TO READ

Eyewitness: Civil War
John Stanchak
Dorling Kindersley (2011)
A visual guide to the weapons and troops, from the birth of the Confederacy to Reconstruction.

The Red Badge of Courage
Stephen Crane
Oxford Paperbacks (1895, 2008)
This classic American novel set in the Civil War describes the fears and experiences of a young soldier fighting in battle.

Atlas of the Civil War
Stephen G Hyslop
National Geographic (2009)
A comprehensive guide to the Civil War, its tactics, armies and battlefields.

Harriet Tubman, Secret Agent : How Daring Slaves and Free Blacks spied for the Union During the Civil War
Thomas B Allan
National Geographic (2009)
The incredible life of Harriet Tubman and her work during the Civil War.

★ MUSEUMS AND WEBSITES TO VISIT

National Civil War Museum
One Lincoln Circle
Harrisburg, PA 17103
www.nationalcivilwarmuseum.org
A comprehensive museum telling the story of the Civil War from both sides.

National Museum of Civil War Medicine
48 East Patrick Street
Frederick, MD 21705
A guide to the medical innovations that resulted from the Civil War.

WEBSITES

Because of the changing nature of Internet links, Rosen Publishing has developed an online list of websites related to the subject of this book. This site is updated regularly. Please use this link to access this list:

http://www.rosenlinks.com/INNO/Civil

INDEX